Original title:
One Day at a Time

Copyright © 2024 Swan Charm
All rights reserved.

Author: Liina Liblikas
ISBN HARDBACK: 978-9916-79-191-2
ISBN PAPERBACK: 978-9916-79-192-9
ISBN EBOOK: 978-9916-79-193-6

The Light of Today

In dawn's embrace, a new day shines,
God's grace ignites the path we tread.
With every step, hope intertwines,
His love surrounding, gently fed.

Through trials faced, we find our way,
Each moment counts, and hearts align.
Faith gathers strength, come what may,
In His light, our spirits twine.

Daily Bread of Grace

With humble hearts, we seek and ask,
For daily joy, for peace to share.
In every prayer, a loving task,
The gifts of faith beyond compare.

Our souls are fed by words divine,
In unity, we grow and strive.
He blesses all, as stars align,
In sacred bond, we stay alive.

Whispered Prayers of Now

In quiet moments, voices blend,
A tender plea, a soulful sigh.
Each whispered prayer, our hearts extend,
To heaven's gate, where hopes can fly.

With every breath, we raise our hands,
And touch the sky with faith anew.
He understands our silent stands,
In love, we find what's ever true.

Faith's Gentle Journey

As rivers flow, our hearts will roam,
Through valleys low, to mountains high.
In faith, we find a distant home,
With every step, our spirits fly.

The road is long, but grace is clear,
Each moment a blessing to embrace.
Through joy and pain, we persevere,
In faith's sweet dance, we know His grace.

Whispers of the Divine

In silence, hearts begin to speak,
Softly calling, spirits seek.
Light cascades through shadows grey,
Guiding souls along their way.

Angels sing on wings of grace,
Offering love, a warm embrace.
In each tear, a prayer is found,
Divine whispers gently surround.

Sacred Threads of Time

Woven in the fabric bright,
Threads of fate in sacred light.
Moments cherished, visions shared,
In each heartbeat, love declared.

Time transcends both space and place,
Echoing the Creator's grace.
Every challenge, every trial,
Threads entwined, a holy dial.

A Blessing in Each Breath

Each inhale, a gift bestowed,
In exhale, worries erode.
Life's rhythm, a sacred dance,
Breath of spirit, our true chance.

From the depths, a prayer arises,
In stillness, pure joy surprises.
With every breath, we find our way,
A blessing bright in light of day.

Graceful Resilience

Through storms that shake and winds that roar,
Faith stands strong, forevermore.
In every trial, hope ignites,
Resilience shines through darkened nights.

With open hearts, we rise anew,
Embracing paths, both bold and true.
Grace sustains in times of strife,
In our trials, we find life.

Cherishing the Here and Now

In the quiet of the dawn,
Let our spirits rise and soar.
Every heartbeat a soft hymn,
Each breath a whisper, adore.

Sunlight dances on the trees,
Golden rays through leaves resound.
Life's a gift, a gentle breeze,
In the now, our peace is found.

Stars above in velvet night,
Guide our hearts to humble prayer.
In each moment, pure delight,
Here and now, our souls lay bare.

As we gather hand in hand,
With love's light, we stand as one.
In this sacred, blessed land,
Cherish all that's just begun.

Life unfolds in quiet grace,
Each moment treasured, divine.
In our hearts, His love we trace,
Cherishing this gift of time.

Each Moment a Song of Praise

In the stillness, hear the call,
Each moment, a note so true.
Life's a canvas, bright and small,
Painted with Him, love anew.

Every laughter, every tear,
An anthem rising, bold and clear.
In the valleys and the heights,
Melodies of grace ignite.

From the morning's gentle light,
To the stars that pierce the night,
Let each heartbeat sing His grace,
In our journey, find our place.

Time, a river flowing free,
Guides us on this sacred path.
Every moment, pure decree,
Reflections of our Savior's wrath.

In His arms, we learn to sing,
Each moment, a cherished thread.
Join our voices, praises ring,
In His love, we are led.

Hearts United in the Now

In the circle of the light,
Hearts entwined in purest grace.
Together we share the fight,
In this sacred, holy space.

Voices lifted, hands held high,
Unified in prayer and hope.
In His love, we cannot lie,
Bound together, we can cope.

Every heartbeat sings of peace,
In his presence, fears release.
Now and always, we are blessed,
In His love, we find our rest.

Moments shared, a timeless bond,
In the now, our spirits rise.
In His mercy, we respond,
Hearts united, one in Christ.

Life a journey, intertwined,
In these moments, truth we find.
With each breath, a prayer sent forth,
In His love, we trace our worth.

The Sacredness of Ordinary Hours

In the stillness of the day,
Find the grace in humble things.
Each moment holds a soft sway,
Like a bird, in praise it sings.

Coffee brewed at morning's light,
Every sip a prayer of thanks.
In the routine, find the bright,
Ordinary, sacred ranks.

Gardens bloom, the flowers sway,
Nature's beauty, pure delight.
In these hours, we learn to pray,
Find His presence day and night.

Evening whispers to the dawn,
As shadows stretch, our hearts ignite.
In these moments, love goes on,
Every second feels so right.

Life's a tapestry of grace,
Woven with the threads we share.
In the ordinary, find your place,
In each hour, a love laid bare.

The Quiet Power of Now

In silence we find, the whispers of grace,
The gentle reminder, of our sacred space.
Breath in the stillness, let worries be free,
In this present moment, we find who we're meant to be.

With hearts open wide, we seek the divine,
In every soft shadow, His light will shine.
A touch of the Spirit, a glance from above,
In the quiet power, we're cradled by love.

Every heartbeat a prayer, each thought a refrain,
Like petals in blossom, we dance in the rain.
Trusting the journey, as time drifts away,
In the quiet power, we learn how to pray.

Wrapped in Today's Embrace

With dawn gently breaking, a promise unfolds,
Each moment a treasure, more precious than gold.
Wrapped in today's embrace, we gather our hope,
In the warmth of His light, together we cope.

Through trials and triumphs, the spirit will guide,
In love's tender arms, we find joy inside.
A tapestry woven, with threads pure and bright,
Wrapped in today's embrace, we rise with the light.

Each step on this path, a sign of His grace,
In laughter and tears, we find our own place.
Blessings like raindrops, they shimmer and flow,
Wrapped in today's embrace, we learn as we grow.

Today's Canvas Painted with Faith

Upon today's canvas, with strokes of our will,
We paint with our actions, our hearts to fulfill.
Each color a moment, each shade a sweet prayer,
Today's canvas painted, with faith everywhere.

The brush of our spirit, in colors so bold,
Crafting our stories, in hues bright and gold.
With faith as our guide, the masterpiece glows,
Today's canvas painted, love endlessly flows.

In shadows and sunlight, we trust and believe,
With grace in our hearts, we learn to receive.
Each day is a gift, with new dreams to chase,
Today's canvas painted, a journey of grace.

Carried by Grace

In the arms of love, we sway,
Guided by light, day by day.
Through trials faced, we find our way,
Carried by grace, come what may.

With every breath, His mercy near,
In moments still, we shed our fear.
A faithful heart, forever dear,
Carried by grace, we persevere.

The gentle whisper of His call,
In shadows cast, we rise, we fall.
Yet in His strength, we will stand tall,
Carried by grace, through it all.

Each step we take, a path divine,
In perfect peace, His love will shine.
In every heart, His truth align,
Carried by grace, forever mine.

So let us walk, in trust and faith,
With every dawn, a new embrace.
In holy love, our souls lay wraith,
Carried by grace, we find our place.

Daily Grace Unfolding

Each morning comes, a gift so bright,
In quiet prayer, we seek His light.
With humble hearts, we start anew,
Daily grace unfolding, pure and true.

As sunbeams break, upon the land,
In gentle hands, we take our stand.
With open arms, His love we find,
Daily grace unfolding, intertwined.

Through trials faced, in whispered prayer,
We lift our hopes, our burdens share.
In every step, He's close behind,
Daily grace unfolding, intertwined.

In loving kindness, we are drawn,
With faith renewed, each heavy yawn.
A testament, in each kind deed,
Daily grace unfolding, our true creed.

So let us rise, with hearts ablaze,
Embracing life, in all its ways.
In grateful song, our voices raise,
Daily grace unfolding, all our days.

The Essence of Today

In stillness found, we seek His face,
The essence blooms in sacred space.
Where every heartbeat echoes love,
The essence of today, from above.

In gentle moments, time stands still,
As we align with His perfect will.
With grateful hearts and voices sway,
The essence of today, come what may.

Each breath a prayer, a song of grace,
In trials met, we find our place.
In living truth, we see the way,
The essence of today, here to stay.

In service shared, our spirits soar,
Through acts of love, we open doors.
Together as one, we'll find our way,
The essence of today, come what may.

So take a step, in faith abide,
In every tear, He'll be our guide.
Embrace the dawn, in joyful play,
The essence of today, come what may.

Living in His Time

In the tapestry of divine grace,
We find our path, a sacred place.
With every heartbeat, love will chime,
Living in His time, oh so sublime.

Through trials faced, we grow and learn,
In patience deep, our hearts will yearn.
With trusting hearts, we start to climb,
Living in His time, our faith will burn.

Through valleys low, and mountains high,
In every tear, His love draws nigh.
With steadfast hope, we rise, we find,
Living in His time, our hearts aligned.

In joy and sorrow, side by side,
Through every storm, in Him we bide.
With open hearts, we seek to bind,
Living in His time, love intertwined.

So let us walk with grace each day,
In every moment, come what may.
In perfect peace, our souls will rhyme,
Living in His time, forever shining.

Serene Steps of Belief

In the quiet dawn of day,
We find the path to grace,
Each gentle breath we take,
Guiding hearts in faith's embrace.

With every step upon this ground,
We walk with love, our spirits soar,
The whispers of the sacred sound,
Inviting us to seek and explore.

In the shadowed vale of doubt,
Hope lights the way like a star,
Through trials that we face without,
We rise above, no matter how far.

Hand in hand with those we meet,
Together we embrace the light,
In every heart, a steady beat,
Reminds us faith will shine so bright.

So take a step, this journey true,
Each moment unfolds divine,
In serene trust, we are renewed,
As love and faith forever intertwine.

Quiet Acts of Faith

In silence soft, a heart will pray,
With humble hands extended wide,
Each act of kindness lights the way,
Through which His love does gently guide.

A smile shared across the room,
A listening ear for one in need,
In such small ways, dispelling gloom,
We plant the everlasting seed.

Each moment spent in silent grace,
Reflects the love in heavens bright,
In every step, we find a place,
To carry hope and share the light.

Through trials faced, we choose to stand,
With faith unyielding and hearts pure,
For in our God, we understand,
With quiet acts, our souls endure.

So let your life a beacon be,
In every act, let love create,
With quiet faith, the world will see,
The light of hope that conquers fate.

Grace in Every Moment

In every breath, a gift of light,
A chance to love, to stand and share,
With grace descending from the height,
We grasp each moment, aware.

Through trials faced and mountains high,
We find the strength to rise anew,
In whispered prayers that touch the sky,
Grace leads us, ever faithful and true.

In laughter shared and tears that fall,
We witness life in all its forms,
His presence felt in every call,
In gentle winds, in vibrant storms.

As seasons shift and time goes by,
Our hearts, resilient, find their beat,
In every moment, we rely,
On love's embrace, so warm and sweet.

With grateful hearts, let praises sing,
In every sunrise, hope is found,
For grace we seek, like birds on wing,
Will lift us high above the ground.

Steps of Faith

With every step along this path,
We tread on ground where angels lay,
In faith, we find the freedom's path,
To walk with grace through night and day.

Though shadows loom and doubts may rise,
We trust the voice that speaks within,
For in our hearts, the truth replies,
That love will guide us through the din.

In moments small, the spirit grows,
A helping hand, a gentle word,
Through simple acts, His mercy flows,
The song of faith is truly heard.

As we ascend these rocky climbs,
With steadfast hearts, we journey on,
In every breath, our souls' wild rhymes,
Will echo love when hope seems gone.

So take a step and feel the ground,
For each footfall brings us near,
In faith's embrace, we are unbound,
The path ahead is ever clear.

Steps of Humble Faith

In quiet stillness, hearts align,
We tread the path, Your light divine.
With every step, we seek Your grace,
In humble faith, we find our place.

With open hands, we feel the call,
In trust, we rise, we will not fall.
Each faltering move, Your love sustains,
Through trials faced, our spirit gains.

A whispered prayer in dark of night,
Awakens hope, renewed in sight.
With simple hearts, we dream anew,
In faith profound, we walk with You.

The smallest seed can grow so tall,
In faith, we answer to Your call.
Together bound, with hearts ablaze,
We share our journey, sing Your praise.

The Promise of This Moment

In every breath, a promise swells,
In silence deep, Your story tells.
This fleeting time, a sacred space,
Embrace the now, seek Your face.

With open eyes, we dare to see,
The wonders great, the mysteries.
In tender light, our spirits soar,
Each heartbeat whispers: love, explore.

Tomorrow's dreams may fade away,
Yet what is ours, we hold today.
With grateful hearts, we lift our voice,
In this moment, we rejoice.

Let gratitude flow like a stream,
In every heart, a vibrant dream.
Each moment shines, a diamond bright,
In love, the promise of the light.

Yesterday's Lessons, Today's Gifts

In shadows cast, we learn and grow,
Each trial faced, a gift to show.
With every stumble, wisdom rains,
From yesterday, our strength remains.

We gather threads of joy and pain,
In life's design, is love's refrain.
With open hearts, we can forgive,
Each lesson learned, a chance to live.

With gentle hands, we shape today,
Embracing gifts along the way.
Each smile shared, a sacred bond,
In unity, we respond.

The past informs the steps we take,
In every choice, new paths we make.
So let us walk with grace and light,
Embracing love and casting fright.

A Tapestry of Today

We weave together threads of grace,
In every moment, a sacred space.
With colors bright, our stories blend,
In life's great tapestry, we mend.

Each laughter shared, a shining thread,
In joy and sorrow, we are led.
With every knot, a lesson learned,
In love's embrace, we are returned.

The fabric stretches, pulls, and sways,
In time's embrace, we find our ways.
Each heartbeat echoes with the past,
Embracing moments made to last.

Together strong, our hopes unite,
In the tapestry, we find our light.
So let us weave with hearts sincere,
A life of love, devoid of fear.

The Promise of Today

Each dawn unfolds a gift so bright,
The sun ascends to chase the night.
With every breath, our hearts obey,
Embracing all the promise of today.

In moments small, His love does bloom,
A whisper soft dispels the gloom.
With faith, we walk the path displayed,
Embracing all the promise of today.

The skies may weep, the storms may roar,
Yet in His hands, we find our core.
Through trials faced and choices made,
Embracing all the promise of today.

His grace, a river strong and wide,
Flows through our fears, our fears subside.
In every challenge, we're unafraid,
Embracing all the promise of today.

So let us rise with hearts renewed,
To spread His love, our souls imbued.
In unity, our voices played,
Embracing all the promise of today.

Spirit's Gentle Guidance

In quiet whispers we shall find,
The Spirit's hand, both soft and kind.
With each step forward, light displayed,
Led by the Spirit's gentle guidance.

Through valleys deep and mountains high,
The sacred voice will never lie.
When shadows loom, be not afraid,
Led by the Spirit's gentle guidance.

In silence deep, He speaks our name,
A flickering flame, yet always the same.
With trust, our hearts shall not be swayed,
Led by the Spirit's gentle guidance.

And when the road seems hard to tread,
Remember love's embrace instead.
In every moment, hope displayed,
Led by the Spirit's gentle guidance.

So walk we shall in faith's embrace,
With every heartbeat, seek His grace.
United, our hearts are not delayed,
Led by the Spirit's gentle guidance.

Finding Peace in the Now

Beneath the noise, a stillness calls,
In sacred spaces, love enthralls.
With open hearts, in grace we bow,
    Finding peace in the now.

Each breath a prayer, a chance to be,
In moments close, we feel Him free.
In every heartbeat, truth allows,
    Finding peace in the now.

The worries fade, like shadows cast,
As faith weaves tapestries vast.
In every presence, take the vow,
    Finding peace in the now.

With hands uplifted, spirits rise,
To touch the heavens, claim the skies.
In love's embrace, we are endowed,
    Finding peace in the now.

Together strong, our voices sing,
A chorus of hope, our souls take wing.
In this sweet moment, here and how,
    Finding peace in the now.

Guided by Faith's Hand

With every step upon this road,
We trust the path our hearts have strode.
In trials faced, we do not strand,
Guided by faith's hand.

Through shadows' depth and light's embrace,
We seek the truth, we seek His face.
In unity, together we stand,
Guided by faith's hand.

Each promise made, a truth will rise,
In storms of life, we claim the skies.
With love as beacon, pure and grand,
Guided by faith's hand.

As rivers flow and seasons change,
Our hearts hold fast, though times are strange.
In every heartbeat, joy is planned,
Guided by faith's hand.

So forward now, with hearts ablaze,
In fervent faith, we sing His praise.
Together bound, we understand,
Guided by faith's hand.

Acts of Faith Unfolding

In shadows deep, our spirits rise,
With whispered prayers towards the skies.
Each deed of love, a guiding light,
In faith we walk, dispelling night.

Through trials faced, our strength we find,
In acts of grace, our hearts aligned.
Together bound, we share this road,
In unity, we bear the load.

With every step, a truth revealed,
In sacred trust, our wounds are healed.
A tapestry of hope we weave,
In giving all, we truly believe.

From ancient texts, the wisdom flows,
As seeds of kindness gently grow.
In service done, our spirits soar,
In faith's embrace, we seek for more.

In every moment, divine we feel,
Through acts of love, our souls reveal.
A journey blessed, we take in stride,
In faith unbound, we shall abide.

The Quiet Call of the Heart

In silence deep, the spirit speaks,
A gentle guide, the heart it seeks.
With every beat, the truth we hear,
In quiet love, we draw so near.

Amid the noise, a sacred peace,
In listening deep, our worries cease.
Through whispered hopes, our souls unite,
In stillness found, we touch the light.

The pathways soft, where shadows dwell,
In heartfelt courage, we break the shell.
With open hearts, we share the dream,
In love's embrace, we find our theme.

Every breath, a sacred song,
In harmony, we all belong.
Through trials faced, we rise above,
In quiet calls, we find our love.

In moments brief, the truth we glean,
A journey shared, in love serene.
With each heartbeat, a prayer we start,
In calm repose, the quiet heart.

A Journey Through This Hour

In every tick, a moment waits,
With open hearts, we contemplate.
The trials faced, the blessings known,
In fleeting time, our seeds are sown.

Through valleys deep and mountains high,
We trust the path, beneath the sky.
Each step we take, a lesson learned,
In every fall, a flame is burned.

A prayer uplifted, the spirit's song,
In unity, we all belong.
With every dawn, new hope we find,
In faith's embrace, our hearts aligned.

Through whispers soft, the grace descends,
In shared compassion, a journey bends.
From dawn to dusk, the light remains,
In every trial, God's love sustains.

A passage marked by love and grace,
In every hour, we find our place.
Through laughter shared and tears we shed,
In this journey, our souls are fed.

The Unfolding Promise

In every dawn, a promise bright,
With tender hands, we shape the light.
Through trials faced, our spirits rise,
In faith's embrace, we touch the skies.

A journey bold, we take as one,
In love's embrace, our hearts have spun.
Every hope, a seed we plant,
In joy and pain, we learn to chant.

Through whispered dreams, the path unfolds,
In sacred bonds, the truth we hold.
With every breath, a grace bestowed,
In trust we walk, where love has flowed.

Together now, we share the song,
In unity, where we belong.
Through darkened nights, a light appears,
In every heartbeat, we meet our fears.

The promise made, forever true,
In every step, we're born anew.
With opened hearts, the journey stays,
In love's reflection, our spirits blaze.

The Beat of Today's Heart

In every pulse, a whisper sings,
Life's rhythm flows, with hope it brings.
Faith dances softly on the breeze,
The heart beats strong, in love's embrace.

Each moment shines, a gift divine,
Guided footsteps by task and sign.
A hymn of grace in daily strife,
The beat of today, the song of life.

With open hands, we seek the light,
In shadows cast, God's warmth ignites.
Finding strength in tender prayer,
The beat of truth is always there.

As sunbeams touch the waking trees,
Awakening faith brings us to our knees.
In silence found, our spirits soar,
The beat of today we can't ignore.

Let every heartbeat echo strong,
With love as our guide, we journey on.
In every tear, in every smile,
The beat of today, eternal style.

Tranquil Steps on Sacred Ground

With each soft step upon this earth,
We find the path of sacred worth.
In quiet moments, peace unfolds,
Tranquil steps, a story told.

Amidst the trees, a gentle sigh,
Nature speaks, as time floats by.
In whispers sweet, the echoes sound,
Our souls rejoice on sacred ground.

The sun's warm rays, a guiding hand,
Inviting us to understand.
With every breath, we find our place,
Tranquil steps in sacred grace.

Hearts aligned with purpose clear,
Each footfall draws us ever near.
In faith, we walk, in joy we run,
Tranquil steps beneath the sun.

The journey's weave, a sacred thread,
In every corner where angels tread.
With grateful hearts, we tread the way,
Tranquil steps, a bright new day.

The Gift of Morning's Glow

When dawn awakes with gentle light,
It paints the sky, dispels the night.
In colors warm, the world is new,
The gift of morning calls to you.

With every ray, a promise clear,
Hope blossoms bright, dispelling fear.
Each moment gift-wrapped in delight,
The gift of morning shines so bright.

The stillness hums, a sacred sound,
God's presence felt, all around.
In whispered prayers, our spirits rise,
The gift of morning, a sweet surprise.

As birds begin their joyful song,
We gather strength, where we belong.
In gratitude, we lift our voice,
The gift of morning makes us rejoice.

So greet each dawn with open heart,
In each new day, we play our part.
With thankful souls, we onward flow,
Embracing life, the morning's glow.

Finding God in Today's Journey

In paths unknown, we wander wide,
With every turn, God's love our guide.
The journey's length, a sacred quest,
Finding God in every test.

Through valleys low and mountains high,
In quiet strength, we learn to fly.
With faithful hearts, we seek the way,
Finding God in each new day.

In laughter shared or tears that fall,
God's presence felt, embracing all.
In every heart, a spark divine,
Finding God in every sign.

With every soul, a bond so pure,
In unity, we find the cure.
As we tread on, our spirits free,
Finding God in you and me.

So hand in hand, we walk this way,
In love and grace, forever stay.
A journey wrapped in hope and trust,
Finding God in all that's just.

The Strength Found in Stillness

In the quiet, peace resides,
A gentle whisper, God abides.
Upon the soul, His light descends,
In stillness, strength and love transcends.

Beneath the burdens, hope renews,
In silent prayer, our spirit grew.
With every breath, we find our way,
Through tranquil nights and blessed day.

Each moment thunders with His grace,
In hushed embrace, we seek His face.
Through trials faced, we stand upright,
In stillness found, our fears take flight.

The heart knows peace when shadows fall,
In solitude, we heed the call.
For in His love, we learn to rest,
In stillness, we are truly blessed.

With open hearts, we find the key,
To harmony and clarity.
In every pause, His voice we hear,
In stillness, love will draw us near.

An Offering of Today's Gratitude

I rise each morn to skies so bright,
With thankful heart, my spirit's light.
For every breath, a gift divine,
My soul in grace, forever shine.

The laughter shared, the trials faced,
In each moment, love embraced.
With grateful hands, I lift my praise,
For simple joys and endless days.

The sun that warms, the rain that falls,
In nature's hymn, the spirit calls.
Each fleeting hour, a treasure true,
In gratitude, my heart renews.

In kindness given and received,
In every moment, I believe.
For life's sweet song, I humbly sing,
In gratitude, my spirit springs.

So let my heart and words align,
In every prayer, Your love, I find.
Today I offer, without shame,
A heart ablaze, in Jesus' name.

Breath of Serenity

In every breath, a sacred gift,
In troubled times, our spirits lift.
A deep inhale, a gentle sigh,
In breath of peace, our worries die.

From chaos springs a quiet grace,
In stillness, we behold His face.
With every heartbeat, love's embrace,
In breath of peace, we find our place.

The moments pause, the world stands still,
Each whispered prayer, our hearts fulfill.
In gentle waves, the spirit flows,
In breath of peace, our calmness grows.

With trust in Him, we breathe anew,
In every sigh, His love shines through.
A rhythm soft, our souls entwine,
In breath of peace, His love divine.

So let each breath be pure and true,
A fleeting gift that guides us through.
In breath of peace, our spirits soar,
In quiet grace, we seek Him more.

Holding Hope in the Now

In this moment, hope's embrace,
A flicker of light in endless space.
With faith unyielding, we stand tall,
In every trial, through it all.

The future waits, yet here we stand,
In love's sweet presence, hand in hand.
With hearts aflame, we trust and see,
In hope's embrace, we shall be free.

Each dawn's new light brings promise near,
With every breath, we cast out fear.
In sacred moments, we are whole,
In faith and love, we find our role.

From ashes rise, our spirits soar,
In hope's warm glow, we seek for more.
With open hearts, we greet the day,
In hope's embrace, we find the way.

So let each moment's light unfold,
In hope's sweet song, our hearts behold.
For in the now, we rise and strive,
In faith and love, we truly thrive.

Faith's Gentle Whisper

In the quiet of the dawn, we seek,
A voice that soothes, a love unique.
Through storms and trials, hope remains,
In faith's embrace, our spirit gains.

With every prayer, a seed is sown,
In hearts united, we're never alone.
Guided by light, we rise and stand,
Hand in hand, we know His plan.

The whispers of grace, soft and true,
Remind us of paths paved anew.
In silence, strength begins to swell,
With each soft word, our souls compel.

Embracing struggle, we find our way,
Trusting the promise of the day.
With every heartbeat, love's refrain,
In faith's gentle whisper, peace we gain.

Through shadows cast by doubt and fear,
We listen closely; His voice is near.
In every moment, joy takes flight,
Bound by love, we bask in light.

Steps of Serenity

In the stillness, hearts align,
Walking paths where love does shine.
Each step a prayer, each breath a song,
Together in faith, we all belong.

The road may twist, the journey long,
Yet in our hearts, we find the strong.
With gentle hopes, we pave our way,
Steps of serenity guide each day.

Guided by stars, we find our place,
In every stumble, there's boundless grace.
With faith as our compass, we embrace,
The tranquil journey, a sacred space.

In moments fleeting, peace we find,
A quiet spirit, a loving mind.
Each tender glance, a bridge we build,
With every step, our hearts are filled.

So let us walk, while spirits soar,
With faith and love, forevermore.
In unity, we rise and sing,
Steps of serenity, our lasting spring.

Abiding in the Moment

In the present, we breathe and dwell,
Each heartbeat a story, a sacred spell.
Moments fleeting, yet deeply felt,
In life's embrace, our fears are dealt.

With open hearts, we learn to see,
The beauty around, passion set free.
In laughter and love, we find the light,
Abiding in moments, pure and bright.

With gratitude sown in every day,
In simple joys, we find our way.
Through trials faced, and dreams ahead,
Faith anchors us, where love is spread.

In whispered prayers, our spirits rise,
We anchor in truth, beyond the skies.
Each moment cherished, woven tight,
Abiding in the moment, we find our might.

With purpose clear, we weave our fate,
In every breath, a chance to create.
Together we seek, our hearts in tune,
In the sacred now, we rise like the moon.

Solitary Grace

In solitude, we find our space,
A quiet heart, a calm embrace.
The world outside may hum and race,
Yet in stillness, we feel His grace.

With whispered thoughts, we turn within,
Where strength renews, and fears grow thin.
In every shadow, light will trace,
In moments spent in solitary grace.

Through silence deep, our spirits soar,
In the hush, we hear the core.
Embracing peace, our hearts interlace,
In solitude, we find our place.

With every tear, a lesson learned,
In hearts ablaze, a fire burned.
With faith held high, we seek His face,
And find our solace in this grace.

The journey inward, a sacred quest,
Where hearts awaken, seeking rest.
In solitary grace, love's warm embrace,
We are all one, in this timeless space.

In the Midst of Each Hour

In the midst of each hour, we gather to pray,
Offering whispers to guide our way.
Hearts intertwined in a sacred embrace,
Finding our solace in love's gentle grace.

With each tick of the clock, His presence is near,
In silence and chaos, we draw ever clear.
Life's fleeting moments, our spirits ignite,
Illuminated paths in the depths of the night.

Breaking bread, we share our deep truth,
In laughter and tears, we honor our youth.
Echoes of faith seep through every large door,
Welcoming blessings, the rich and the poor.

In hymns that resound, our hopes take their flight,
Hands clasped together, we shine as the light.
In the church of our hearts, a shelter divine,
Forever bound in His love, ever entwined.

Faithful Heartbeats

Each heartbeat a prayer, a rhythm divine,
A song of devotion that echoes through time.
In every soft breath, His presence we find,
Faithful and constant, our spirits aligned.

Through valleys of shadow and hills standing tall,
We rise in His grace, in love we shall call.
With eyes open wide, we dance through the night,
In faith we find courage, our hearts shining bright.

With each gentle tear, a story unfolds,
Of mercy and kindness, of love that consoles.
A tapestry woven with threads of the soul,
In grace we discover the beauty of whole.

In the stillness we gather, our hearts intertwined,
A family of spirit, united, aligned.
Through trials and triumphs, in Him we take flight,
Our faithful heartbeats, a beacon of light.

Navigating Today's Waters

Navigating today's waters, we seek His guide,
In currents of chaos, He stands by our side.
With wisdom as anchor, our sails filled with trust,
We journey through storms, in Him we find thrust.

When waves crash around us, our hearts fill with fear,
His voice whispers softly, 'My child, I am near.'
In the midst of the trials, our faith starts to swell,
For love conquers storms, and all will be well.

Through valleys of doubt, we hold to His light,
With hands raised in prayer, we embrace the night.
In the stillness of grace, our spirits take flight,
Transitioning shadows into morning's bright sight.

As waters calm down, we gaze at the shore,
Reflecting on journeys that shape who we are.
With gratitude blooming, we step out in peace,
In faith we find refuge, and strife finds its cease.

Simple Acts of Devotion

In simple acts of devotion, we find our way,
A smile shared, a kind word, a moment to stay.
In the flicker of candles, we offer our prayer,
With open hearts ready, our burdens to share.

The warmth of a glance, the touch of a hand,
In each gentle gesture, together we stand.
With love that transcends, we gather as one,
In harmony's embrace, our journey begun.

Through laughter and giving, our spirits take flight,
In every small moment, we shine love's pure light.
As seasons are changing, we stay rooted in grace,
One act of kindness can shift every space.

Deep breaths in the silence, a prayer softly said,
Inviting His blessings, our worries shed.
With hearts wide open, we step forth in trust,
In simple acts of devotion, we flourish and rust.

Each Hour a Gift

In every hour, blessings unfold,
Moments of grace, treasures untold.
We seek the light, a guiding hand,
In the weave of time, we take our stand.

Awake, aware, in dawn's soft glow,
Each tick a whisper, each second a flow.
With gratitude, our hearts ignite,
In spirit's embrace, we find our light.

Let not the minutes slip away,
Hold tight to love, come what may.
In the rhythm of life, the sacred song,
We find our place, where we belong.

Each heartbeat echoes, divine and near,
A gentle reminder that God is here.
The tapestry of hours, rich and bright,
In faith we walk, into the light.

So cherish each hour, for it is a thread,
Woven with love, where angels tread.
With every gift of time bestowed,
We walk in grace, on heaven's road.

The Stillness Within

In the quiet heart, a whisper sings,
A sacred hush, where spirit springs.
In stillness, truth begins to shine,
A place of peace, where grace aligns.

Beneath the noise, the chaos, the strife,
Lies a gentle stream, the essence of life.
In meditation, we find our way,
To the calm within, where shadows sway.

The soul's gentle voice, in silence speaks,
To the hungry heart, the spirit seeks.
In the twilight of thoughts, serenity reigns,
In the stillness within, the heart sustains.

Each breath we take, a prayer takes flight,
Woven with love, through the starry night.
In the pause, we learn to be still,
And in that silence, discover His will.

So find your peace in the quiet deep,
A treasure of faith, ours to keep.
For in stillness, we rise and see,
The boundless love that sets us free.

Cherished Moments of Grace

In fleeting time, we grasp the day,
Moments of grace, like dew they lay.
With open hearts and eyes so wide,
We savor life, our gentle guide.

The laughter shared, a soft embrace,
In cherished moments, we find our place.
With every smile, a blessing flows,
In love's pure light, the spirit grows.

Through trials faced, through joys we find,
In every heartbeat, love intertwined.
The sacred now, a gift bestowed,
In cherished grace, our journey glowed.

We walk in faith through every porthole,
Finding joy where spirit consoles.
In each breath's whisper, a prayer we make,
For cherished moments, our hearts awake.

In life's vast tapestry, we take our part,
Each moment treasured, a work of art.
With gratitude, we dance and sing,
In cherished grace, our souls take wing.

In the Embrace of the Present

In the here and now, our spirits meet,
In every heartbeat, in every beat.
Embraced by time, we gather near,
In the present moment, we shed our fear.

Each sunrise speaks of hope renewed,
A sacred space where love's imbued.
In the now we find our way,
Guided by grace, come what may.

Let go of past, the future unknown,
In this embrace, we are never alone.
With open hearts, we choose to see,
The beauty of life, our destiny.

In laughter and tears, the truth resides,
In the present's glow, our faith abides.
With every breath, let peace unfold,
In this embrace, we are consoled.

So hold this moment, a gift divine,
In the embrace of the present, love aligns.
Through each fleeting second, we rise and shine,
In the sacred now, the world is mine.

The Light We Carry

In shadows deep, our spirits yearn,
A guiding flame, within us burns.
With faith as shield, we walk this way,
The light we carry, here to stay.

Through trials fierce, and skies so gray,
We lift our hearts, and humbly pray.
Together strong, through storms we wade,
In every moment, Love's cascade.

The lantern bright, in darkest night,
Reminds our souls, to seek the light.
With gentle whispers, dreams unfold,
Each step we take, a tale retold.

In trust and hope, we find our way,
With every dawn, a new display.
Through valleys low, and mountains high,
Our soaring spirits touch the sky.

Let love's embrace, our hearts entwine,
In joy and sorrow, pure divine.
The light we carry, ever near,
Through every doubt, we persevere.

Journey of the Believer

Upon the road, our feet do tread,
With silent prayers, and tears we've shed.
In search of truth, we wander far,
Each step we take, a guiding star.

Through valleys deep, and mountains steep,
The promises we hold, we keep.
With open hearts, we share the way,
And find our strength in humble sway.

Each soul we meet, a sacred chance,
To weave our hopes in holy dance.
In every trial, and gentle face,
The journey's grace, our hearts embrace.

With faith as compass, love our tune,
We walk together, morning, noon.
Through seasons change, our spirits rise,
In unity, we reach the skies.

So lift your eyes, and trust the path,
In love's sweet hymn, we find our math.
The journey calls, let's boldly steer,
For every step, the Light is near.

Patience's Quiet Song

In quiet stillness, echoes dwell,
A whispered truth, a sacred spell.
With every breath, we learn to wait,
For faith blooms slow; it's never late.

In gentle moments, time expands,
We find our peace in loving hands.
With tender hearts, we navigate,
Each lesson learned, a treasured state.

Through trials tough, and storms that rage,
Patience, our guide, turns every page.
With hopeful whispers, dreams ignite,
In shadows dumb, we seek the light.

Embrace the dawn, with open arms,
For every pause, the Spirit calms.
In stillness found, we hear Love's song,
A melody that makes us strong.

So hold on tight, and trust the flow,
In quiet faith, our spirits grow.
With patience sweet, we face each day,
In time, we find the truest way.

Marshaling the Hours

In briefest moments, life unfolds,
Each hour a thread, a story holds.
With grace we weave, in time's embrace,
A tapestry of love and grace.

The minutes pass, like whispers soft,
In daily toil, our souls take off.
With every tick, we find our role,
Marshalling time, we mark our goal.

In sacred rhythms, hearts align,
For every breath, the stars still shine.
With purpose clear, we live, we strive,
In marshaled hours, our dreams alive.

So gather 'round, and hold on tight,
In shared endeavors, hearts take flight.
For every day, a gift bestowed,
In time's embrace, our love's abode.

Let moments glisten, let them sing,
As life unfolds, by grace we cling.
With each new hour, a chance to grow,
In marshaled time, our spirits glow.

Each Minute a Blessing

In every tick, a chance to see,
The grace that flows so endlessly.
With whispered prayers, we rise and fall,
Each moment sacred, Heeding His call.

The sun that shines, the stars so bright,
Are gifts bestowed by love's pure light.
In laughter shared and tears we shed,
Each minute cherished, where angels tread.

From dawn to dusk, let hearts be free,
To dance in joy and harmony.
Embracing life with open hands,
In every breath, His presence stands.

So let us weave our tales of grace,
In time's embrace, find our true place.
With gratitude, our spirits rise,
Each minute a blessing, heaven's prize.

The Weight of Tomorrow Released

Cast off the burdens held so tight,
In faith we walk, guided by light.
The worries of tomorrow fade,
In trusting hearts, His will is laid.

With every breath, release despair,
For in His arms, we find repair.
No yoke of fear can bind us down,
In grace, we wear our victory crown.

For joy awaits in each new dawn,
With hope renewed, the past is gone.
Let every step be blessed with peace,
The weight of tomorrow finds its release.

We walk in steps of loved and prayed,
Through valleys deep, our fears are swayed.
In trust we rise; His strength we find,
The weight of tomorrow left behind.

Living in God's Embrace

In every heartbeat, His love resides,
An endless river, where peace abides.
Through trials faced, we've come to know,
In God's embrace, our spirits grow.

The mountains high and valleys low,
In His warm light, our faith will glow.
When storms may rage and shadows loom,
His gentle presence sweeps the room.

Each whispered prayer, a guiding spark,
In darkest nights, He lights the dark.
With open arms, He welcomes all,
In joy and sorrow, hear His call.

Together we walk, we're never lost,
In love's embrace, we count the cost.
For every moment spent in grace,
Is living true in God's embrace.

Trusting in the Now

In present moments, we find our peace,
Letting go of worry, finding release.
With faith as our guide, we journey on,
Trusting in the now, a brand new dawn.

Each breath a promise, each step a song,
In love's sweet cadence, we truly belong.
The past has faded, the future unseen,
In faith's gentle arms, we're ever keen.

The beauty of living, it starts today,
In simple joys, we find His way.
With hearts open wide, we'll cherish each hour,
Trusting in the now, His love, our power.

For every moment is a gift divine,
In the tapestry of life, His hand we find.
So let us dance, unburdened in light,
Trusting in the now, our spirits take flight.

Peaceful Pilgrimage

In quiet pathways, we find our way,
With every step, our hearts do sway.
The whispers of hope lead us on,
Towards dawn's light, where sorrows are gone.

With faith as our guide, we sing along,
In sacred silence, we feel so strong.
Every stone and leaf, a story told,
In nature's embrace, where love unfolds.

We seek the truth in each gentle breeze,
Finding solace beneath the trees.
Hands lifted high, our spirits rise,
In unity, we touch the skies.

Through valleys deep and mountains high,
Our journey painted with a sigh.
In every shadow, light will find,
A purpose clear, a path designed.

With every heartbeat, we feel the call,
To stand together, to never fall.
A peaceful pilgrimage, hand in hand,
In this sacred journey, we take a stand.

Moments of Reverence

In stillness, we gather, hearts ablaze,
In moments of reverence, we lift our gaze.
Each breath a prayer, a sacred bond,
In unity we cherish, we respond.

The echoes of faith, like soft refrain,
Remind us gently of joy and pain.
In the hush of the dawn, we seek the light,
With open hearts, we embrace the night.

A tapestry woven with threads of grace,
In divine presence, we find our place.
With gratitude deep, we gather near,
Finding strength in love, casting out fear.

Through fragrant fields and rivers wide,
Moments of reverence, our hearts abide.
In this holy dance, we find our truth,
Together, radiant in eternal youth.

With hands entwined and spirits free,
In sacred moments, we long to be.
Embracing the mystery of life's design,
In every heartbeat, a love divine.

Light in Each Footstep

As I walk the path of faith's embrace,
I carry your light, a sacred space.
In every footstep, grace falls anew,
Guiding my way, in all that I do.

With stars to guide and trees to lean,
The beauty of existence, serene and keen.
I whisper my dreams to the moonlit night,
And find in darkness, the promise of light.

Each trial faced, a lesson learned,
In humble hearts, the fire is burned.
With patience and love, we forge ahead,
Trusting the path where angels tread.

Through winding roads and whispers of prayer,
In each footstep, we find love's care.
Together we journey, shadows behind,
Towards horizons where hearts intertwine.

With open hearts, we journey on,
Embracing each moment, dusk till dawn.
Light in each footstep, warm and bright,
Leading us home, through day and night.

Faithful Heartbeats

In the rhythm of life, our spirits soar,
With faithful heartbeats, we seek for more.
In every challenge, a lesson deep,
With love as our anchor, faith we keep.

Through stormy nights and sunlit days,
We walk with courage, our hearts ablaze.
In whispers of hope, we find our way,
With each faithful heartbeat, come what may.

Together we rise, united in grace,
In the dance of existence, we find our place.
With voices raised, we sing our song,
In the heart of the world, where we belong.

Amidst the trials, we find the light,
Through valleys of sorrow, we journey bright.
With every heartbeat, truth will unfold,
In the warmth of faith, our story is told.

In quiet moments and joyous cheer,
Faithful heartbeats, forever near.
Together we stand, unshaken, bold,
In the embrace of love, our hearts unfold.

Divine Imprints of Today

In the dawn's gentle light, we rise anew,
Each step we take, a promise so true.
With faith as our guide, we walk the way,
Grateful for blessings that fill our day.

In every smile, in every embrace,
We find the whispers of divine grace.
Through trials faced, we learn and grow,
With love in our hearts, we let it show.

Nature's splendor reveals His hand,
In mountains tall and in soft, warm sand.
We see His work in the skies so vast,
A reminder of love that forever will last.

When shadows linger, and doubts arise,
We lift our eyes to the endless skies.
For in the silence, His presence we find,
A light that guides and a peace that binds.

Today we cherish, tomorrow we claim,
Each moment a spark in His holy name.
With hearts set aflame, we worship and pray,
To honor the imprints of this sacred day.

Harvesting Joy in Today's Fields

In fields of grace, we sow our seeds,
With hands uplifted to meet the needs.
Each moment spent in joyful toil,
Brings forth the blessings from rich, soft soil.

The sun shines bright on paths we tread,
With faith as a compass, where love is spread.
In laughter and song, we gather the grain,
Harvesting joy through sunshine and rain.

With every breath, we embrace the day,
In sharing our hearts, we find our way.
The fruits of kindness, love's sweet embrace,
Filling our souls with divine grace.

The labor may weary, but hearts stay strong,
For in this work, we all belong.
Together we rise, as one we stand,
The joy of the harvest held close at hand.

So let us gather with grateful hearts,
In all that we do, each day imparts.
To honor the fields where love's bounty lies,
In the beauty of life, our spirits rise.

The Still Small Voice

In the quiet moments, He speaks to me,
A gentle whisper, setting my heart free.
Through trials and storms, His words I seek,
For in the silence, it's hope I speak.

When chaos reigns and loud voices call,
His still small voice bids me not to fall.
In solitude's peace, my soul feels whole,
For love's soft cadence is balm to my soul.

Through prayerful thoughts and a heart attuned,
I find my strength in the love He's crooned.
Each breath I take is a sacred chance,
To linger in trust and in holy dance.

In valleys low, and on mountains high,
I listen intently, to His soft sigh.
For in every moment, He walks beside,
Guiding my heart with the love He provides.

May I always heed that voice so slight,
Trailing beside me, a shimmering light.
In faith I follow, through dark and bright,
The still small voice is my heart's true rite.

A Promise Renewed Each Morning

With every sunrise, a promise unfolds,
A whisper of hope in the heart it holds.
Each new dawn brings a chance to arise,
To seek out the light in the endless skies.

In the dew-kissed grass, the world awakes,
With blessings to gather, a joy that makes.
As shadows retreat and darkness departs,
His love shines through, igniting our hearts.

We tread on the path He lays before,
With faith as our anchor, forevermore.
Each step is a vow, a chance to renew,
In the arms of grace, we find the true view.

As prayers ascend like petals in flight,
We celebrate life, in His wondrous light.
The promise of love, unwavering and clear,
A beacon of hope, throughout the year.

So let us embrace each gift that we find,
With peace in our souls and love intertwined.
For every morning brings forth the gift,
Of promises renewed, our spirits uplift.

Joys Untold in Each Sunrise

The dawn breaks forth with grace,
Unveiling colors bright and pure.
Whispers of hope fill the air,
Each morning brings a heart's allure.

The sun ascends, a sacred fire,
Chasing shadows far away.
In its light, our souls aspire,
To greet the joys of each new day.

With every ray, a promise shines,
A chance for love, and peace, and praise.
In nature's hymn, our spirit binds,
To revel in the divine ways.

Our hearts rejoice, for blessings flow,
In every breath, we find our worth.
The beauty of creation's glow,
Awakens joy throughout the earth.

As we behold the rising sphere,
Let gratitude within us swell.
For joys untold are ever near,
In sunrise's arms, we find our well.

The Power of Present Praise

In quiet moments, hearts align,
With whispers soft, we lift our voice.
In every beat, a chance to shine,
With present praise, we make our choice.

Let not the past weigh down our song,
For each new breath brings grace anew.
In simple words, we all belong,
And find the strength to see it through.

The power lies in now, so clear,
In gratitude, we rise and stand.
We worship here, with love sincere,
In every heartbeat, God's command.

The melodies of life unfold,
In moments shared, we feel His love.
With voices raised, we sing of gold,
The present praise, a gift from above.

So here we gather, hand in hand,
Rejoicing in the light we bring.
With every word, a promise planned,
In power of praise, our spirits sing.

Reflections in the Mirror of Today

In every glance, a story told,
The mirror shows what lies within.
Each moment's truth, both meek and bold,
Reflects the light where love begins.

We ponder choices made before,
And lift our gaze to all we see.
In every trial, each open door,
The mirror beckons, guiding me.

Today's reflections shape our heart,
In wisdom gained through paths we tread.
Embracing life as sacred art,
We find the peace where spirits led.

So let us gaze with tender grace,
Embracing flaws that make us whole.
In love's embrace, we find our place,
Reflected truth ignites the soul.

For in the mirror's quiet glow,
We are reminded, flesh and clay.
Each day a chance to love and grow,
In reflections of this sacred way.

Suitcase of Today's Blessings

In a suitcase worn, we carry dreams,
Packed tightly with our hopes and fears.
Each blessing shines, like sunlit beams,
A testament to countless years.

What treasures lie within this case?
The laughter shared, the love bestowed.
Each memory a gentle grace,
A guide along this winding road.

With every step, we feel the weight,
Of gratitude each day unfolds.
In trials faced, we contemplate,
The deeper joys that life enfolds.

So let us open wide the seams,
And share the treasures held so dear.
For in the sharing of these dreams,
We find the light that draws us near.

This suitcase holds our lives combined,
A tapestry of faith and love.
In every blessing, light is twined,
A glimpse of heaven here above.

Trust and Tread Softly

In whispers soft, the Spirit speaks,
Where shadows dance and truth still seeks.
With humble hearts, we seek the light,
And tread with care, through day and night.

Each step we take, a sacred vow,
In faith we rise, and here, we bow.
For trust in Him will guide our way,
Each whispered prayer, a bright array.

In valleys low, when spirits wane,
He lifts us high, relieves our pain.
With gentle hands, He molds our hopes,
In silent love, our heart elopes.

Through trials fierce, our souls will soar,
For in His grace, we find much more.
So tread softly, with faith so bold,
In whispers sweet, His love unfolds.

With every dawn, His mercies new,
We trust in Him, in all we do.
Together we walk, in joy and strife,
In every heartbeat, there's a life.

Moments of Faith

In moments brief, we catch His gaze,
A flicker bright, through endless haze.
With grateful hearts, we bow and sing,
In fleeting time, His praises cling.

Each moment holds a sacred grace,
In every trial, we find our place.
With open palms, we lift our needs,
In trust, we plant the hopeful seeds.

The quiet whispers of the night,
Transport our fears into the light.
In gentle dawn, renewal comes,
Our hearts aglow, the Spirit drums.

Though storms may rise and shadows fall,
We stand as one, we heed His call.
With every breath, our faith renews,
In every moment, love imbues.

So cherish now, each fleeting breath,
For in this time, we find our depth.
In moments shared, we rise above,
Together woven, bound by love.

The Path of the Present

Upon this path, the present lies,
Where hope ignites, and faith complies.
Each footstep firm, on sacred ground,
In silence sweet, His grace is found.

With every turn, a lesson learned,
In laughter's joy and sorrow's burned.
The moment calls, we heed its sound,
In present time, His love is found.

Amidst the noise, His voice is clear,
A guiding light, dispelling fear.
With every heartbeat, faith takes flight,
In every tear, we find our sight.

As seasons change and shadows drift,
Our hearts align, our spirits lift.
Embrace the now, for here we see,
In every breath, He dwells in me.

So walk this path, firm and free,
In present grace, our destiny.
For in His love, we find our home,
In every moment, we're never alone.

Each Dawn a Promise

With every dawn, a promise wakes,
In golden hues, our spirit aches.
A new day shines, with hope to spare,
In every breath, His love declared.

He paints the sky with colors bright,
And wraps our hearts in purest light.
Each moment fresh, like morning dew,
In every heartbeat, His love is true.

When shadows fall, and doubts arise,
We chase the dawn, where faith defies.
In every trial, His strength we find,
Our spirits soar, our souls unbind.

Each promise made, a seed that's sown,
In trust we walk, we're never alone.
For every dawn, His grace will shine,
In every heart, His love divine.

So greet the morn, with open arms,
Embrace the light, resist dark charms.
For in each dawn, we find our way,
In every promise, He is our stay.

Moments of Divine Presence

In shadows cast by morning light,
We feel the touch of grace so bright.
In whispers soft, the spirit calls,
In quiet moments, the heart enthralls.

With every dawn, a chance to see,
The hands of love that set us free.
In sacred stillness, truth resides,
In gentle waves, the soul abides.

Beneath the stars, in darkest night,
The spark of hope ignites our plight.
Through trials faced and burdens borne,
In every tear, a promise born.

In laughter shared, and kindness shown,
The beauty of our hearts is grown.
With open arms, the world we greet,
In every stranger, love we meet.

Embrace the now, the fleeting time,
In every moment, joy and rhyme.
A dance of souls, united, pure,
In each divine encounter, we endure.

With Each Breath, a Gift

In each small breath, a treasure lies,
A sacred gift beneath the skies.
With every heartbeat, life sings clear,
A rhythm sweet, a song we hear.

The air we take, a holy grace,
In moments shared, we find our place.
With gratitude, the spirit grows,
In silent awe, our witness flows.

Each breath we share, a bond renewed,
In whispered prayers, our hearts imbued.
With every sigh, release the pain,
In love's embrace, we rise again.

Let each inhale bring wisdom near,
With every exhale, cast out fear.
In the ebb and flow, we shall find,
The peace that dwells within the mind.

With every breath, the promise shines,
In sacred moments, love defines.
Through trials steep, and joy untold,
In every heartbeat, life unfolds.

The Sacred Rhythm of Life

In the gentle sway of trees in prayer,
The rhythm of life dances in the air.
With each new season, change takes flight,
In harmony, we find our light.

The sun that rises, a faithful guide,
The moon that whispers, where hope resides.
In every wave, in every breeze,
A sacred pulse, our hearts appease.

In laughter's echo, in sorrow's ache,
The sacred rhythm, no heart can break.
In every moment, a song unfolds,
Within each story, the truth it holds.

With hands held high, we join the dance,
In unity, we take our stance.
Through trials fierce and victories sweet,
We find the sacred, and love's heartbeat.

So let us sway to this divine beat,
With gratitude, life feels complete.
In every heartbeat, we shall thrive,
In the sacred rhythm, we're alive.

Daily Revelations

In morning light, a promise clear,
Each day unfolds with hope sincere.
In quietude, the spirit speaks,
In humble moments, wisdom peaks.

Each sunrise paints a brand new start,
A canvas fresh for every heart.
With open eyes, we seek the truth,
In every dawn, the spark of youth.

Through trials faced, the lessons learned,
In every turn, the heart is turned.
With every stumble, growth we gain,
In daily revelations, joy and pain.

With gentle grace, the path we tread,
In every challenge, faith is fed.
With every heartbeat, love's embrace,
In daily moments, we find our place.

So let us walk this sacred ground,
In each step taken, peace is found.
With open hearts, the world we greet,
In daily revelations, life is sweet.

Seasons of Solace

In the quiet of dawn, grace unfolds,
Whispers of love in stories told.
Each moment a gift, each breath a sign,
In nature's arms, our hearts align.

Amidst the storms, we seek the light,
In shadows deep, faith takes flight.
With every season, our spirits mend,
In solace found, we walk, we blend.

The springtime blooms in colors bright,
A promise renewed, hope in sight.
Summer's warmth wraps us in peace,
In the harvest's joy, our worries cease.

Autumn leaves like thoughts descend,
In the cycle of life, we comprehend.
Winter's chill, a blanket of grace,
In every season, we find our place.

Together we walk, hand in hand,
Trusting the journey, a sacred strand.
In seasons of solace, love is the key,
Unlocking the bonds of eternity.

Guardian in the Now

In the stillness of now, a whisper calls,
A guardian watchful, within these walls.
Each heartbeat a rhythm, a sacred dance,
Trusting the moment, embracing chance.

The past may linger, the future may gleam,
But in the present, we find our dream.
With open hearts, we heed the way,
Guided by love, come what may.

A light in the darkness, a hope that grows,
In every challenge, a spirit knows.
The pulse of creation, flowing through time,
In gratitude's grace, our souls will climb.

Fear not the shadows, embrace the day,
For the guardian whispers, "You're on your way."
Each breath a blessing, each sigh a prayer,
The journey unfolds, always aware.

With trust unbroken, we rise anew,
In the guardian's gaze, find strength to pursue.
In the now, we gather, ever more free,
Bound by the love that creates harmony.

Rays of Hope

When darkness falls and shadows creep,
Rays of hope begin to seep.
In the cracks where light breaks through,
A promise to hold, a vision anew.

Each dawn brings grace on golden wings,
A symphony of hope, the heartstrings sing.
In every trial, the spirit shines,
For love's gentle touch forever aligns.

Through storms of sorrow, we shall rise,
Lifting our gaze to the endless skies.
In the depths of struggle, we take a stand,
With faith as our guide, we walk hand in hand.

The world may tremble, but we are strong,
In unity's song, we've belonged.
Rays of hope are ours to share,
In kindness and love, we answer prayer.

With hearts aflame, let our voices soar,
For in the light, we find so much more.
Rays of hope ignite the fire,
A beacon of love, our hearts inspire.

Trusting Tomorrow's Grace

In the twilight glow, we learn to trust,
Tomorrow's promise shines through the dust.
With open hands, we release our fears,
Embracing the journey through laughter and tears.

Each step we take, guided by grace,
A rhythm steady, our sacred space.
In the unknown, our spirits soar,
For love will lead us to the open door.

Though paths may twist and turn anew,
In every challenge, our faith will brew.
With hope as the anchor, we face the day,
Trusting tomorrow, come what may.

In silence we gather, our hearts unite,
Bearing witness to the stars so bright.
With courage to journey, together we rise,
In trusting tomorrow, our spirits devise.

As dawn breaks forth with colors ablaze,
We walk in faith, through life's complex maze.
With love as our compass, we'll find our way,
Trusting tomorrow's grace, day by day.

Miracles in the Mundane

In the quiet morn, light ascends,
A simple smile, where hope transcends.
Birds take flight, their songs a prayer,
Whispers of grace, a heart laid bare.

A hidden touch in daily toil,
Threads of kindness, love's fertile soil.
Small blessings found in fleeting time,
In every moment, the divine rhyme.

Rain-drenched petals, beauty revealed,
Nature's touch, our spirits healed.
The laughter of children, pure and bright,
Reminds us all of heaven's light.

In crowded streets, hand in hand,
Strangers unite, despite the land.
Eternal sparks in the common gaze,
Unveiling wonder in ordinary ways.

Each breath a gift, profound and sweet,
In mundane lives, where miracles meet.
Awake, arise, in love abide,
In every heartbeat, God's hand provided.

Embracing the Present

Time flows gently, a sacred thread,
In the now, the spirit is fed.
Let worries fade, like mist in air,
Embrace this moment, pure and rare.

Sunrise paints the sky anew,
Each color speaks of love so true.
Feel the warmth on weary skin,
In these moments, life begins.

Thoughts of tomorrow can weigh us down,
Yet here and now, joy can be found.
In laughter shared, and silence too,
We find our place, as hearts renew.

The breeze carries whispers of grace,
Reminding us to slow our pace.
In the sacred hush, God's love prevails,
Embracing the present, our spirit sails.

With open hearts, we choose to see,
All of today's blessed simplicity.
In gratitude, let our voices sing,
For in each moment, hope takes wing.

Alone but Not Abandoned

In silence deep, the heart does ache,
Yet in the solitude, strength we make.
God walks beside us, though unseen,
In whispered prayers, we are redeemed.

The stars align in darkest nights,
A reminder of love's guiding lights.
Loneliness, a shadow passed,
In sacred presence, peace is cast.

Each tear that falls is not in vain,
A cleansing stream to wash the pain.
The soul's embrace, a gentle hand,
Both fierce and tender, here we stand.

Wounds may ache, but faith will mend,
In this journey, we are friends.
With open arms, the universe calls,
Reminding us love never falls.

Alone we may walk, but never stray,
In the heart's quiet, light will stay.
Eternity's echo in every sigh,
Alone, not abandoned, we learn to fly.

Peace Within Today's Trials

In the storm's eye, calm can be found,
In faith's embrace, our hearts are bound.
Though trials come, like waves on shore,
In peace, we rise, forevermore.

Each burden carried, a lesson taught,
In struggle's grip, wisdom is sought.
The thorns of life may prick and sting,
But through the pain, melodies sing.

We find our strength in grace's fold,
A quiet spirit, courageous and bold.
With every trial, resilience grows,
In the heart's garden, love overflows.

In moments of doubt, breathe and be still,
Let faith arise, let trust fulfill.
For every shadow, light will break,
In peace within, the heart will wake.

Together we stand, through thick and thin,
In life's gentle dance, the peace begins.
Let hope be our anchor, solid and true,
Through trials faced, we are made new.

Daily Strands of Hope

In the dawn of light, we rise anew,
Casting shadows, as sorrows lift,
Each heartbeat whispers, faith shines through,
A tapestry woven, a sacred gift.

Paths uncertain, yet we trust the way,
Guided by grace, we tread the hour,
In every trial, love will convey,
A promise strong, a radiant flower.

Moments fleeting like a gentle breeze,
Hope unfolds in every sigh,
Through each challenge, we find our ease,
As the spirit's song begins to fly.

In every tear, a lesson grown,
In laughter's echo, joy's embrace,
We gather strength, and not alone,
For life's mosaic, divine in grace.

Together we stand, hands intertwined,
Hearts ignited with whispers of truth,
In the fabric of time, love's defined,
Each strand a blessing, eternal youth.

The Grace of Small Things

In petals soft, the dew collects,
A quiet moment, a sacred gaze,
In little wonders, spirit reflects,
Life's simple joys, a quiet blaze.

The rustle of leaves, a whisper divine,
In the gentle warmth of a lover's smile,
A thousand prayer notes, they intertwine,
In each heartbeat, grace walks a mile.

A child's laughter, pure and bright,
Lost in the clouds, a fleeting flight,
In every breath, in day or night,
Love's quiet song, a guiding light.

In the hum of life, the world enshrined,
Moments cherished, so often ignored,
In small things, the great design,
A universe of love, forever poured.

Let us not overlook what the heart brings,
For in humble places, life softly clings,
In the grace of small things, our spirit sings,
In awareness, a treasure that joyously springs.

Hidden Treasures of Today

Look around, what do you see?
In the mundane, miracles lie,
Each fleeting moment, meant to be,
Unveiling treasures, where hearts can fly.

The sun that rises, a painter's hue,
Morning whispers, casting a glow,
Gratitude's path, a journey true,
In each heartbeat, a sacred flow.

In every laugh, a spirit's embrace,
In silence' soft, our souls align,
Treasures hidden in life's gentle pace,
Revealing wonders, divine design.

As shadows dance with the fading light,
Seek the gems that the day has wrought,
In the tender dusk, find your sight,
For hidden treasures are all we sought.

Let go of worries, let love unfold,
In each heartbeat, a promise made,
Today is a story, a tale retold,
In the grace of now, our fears will fade.

Silence Speaks to the Soul

In stillness deep, we find our peace,
A tender hush, where thoughts conflate,
In silence, burdens find release,
And faith unfolds in quiet state.

The world may roar, but here we dwell,
Where whispers of love softly soar,
In the gentle pause, we hear the swell,
Of sacred truths and so much more.

Moments of quiet, our hearts align,
In meditation, the spirit finds home,
In the depths of silence, stars do shine,
Guiding us forth, no need to roam.

For in each breath, a prayer is spun,
In stillness, the soul finds its goal,
Lost in the peace, we are all one,
As silence speaks to the heart and soul.

So let us cherish the hours of grace,
Embrace the stillness, let worries cease,
In silence, a sacred, holy space,
Where love becomes our everlasting peace.

Guided by Faith's Light

In shadows deep, we seek the flame,
A light that calls us by His name.
With steadfast hearts, we walk the way,
Each step in trust, come what may.

The path is bright with love's embrace,
In trials faced, we find His grace.
With every prayer, the spirit soars,
Faith's gentle whisper, forever endures.

Through valleys low and mountains high,
We lift our gaze beyond the sky.
In every moment, hope ignites,
Together walking in His light.

With hands joined tight, we share our fears,
In unity, we dry our tears.
For in His plan, we find our way,
Guided by faith, day by day.

Let love abound in all we do,
A shining beacon, strong and true.
In every heart, let kindness start,
Faith's light shall guide each soul and heart.

A Prayer for the Present

Today we bow, with heads held high,
In gratitude for every sigh.
A moment's breath, a whispered plea,
In stillness, Lord, we turn to Thee.

With open hearts, we seek Your will,
In every task, Your light instill.
In joy and struggle, side by side,
We find our strength, in You we bide.

Let kindness flow, like rivers wide,
In times of doubt, be our guide.
With every heartbeat, let us share,
A love that frees, beyond compare.

As hours pass, we pause and pray,
For peace to reign and hope's display.
In simple acts, Your grace we find,
A prayer for now, with love combined.

May faith sustain in all we face,
In every tear, a touch of grace.
In this brief hour, let us be,
In Every moment, close to Thee.

Every Moment, a Testament

In each small breath, a story lies,
A testament beneath the skies.
Moments pass, yet still remain,
With faith as light, we bear the strain.

In laughter shared, and in our tears,
We witness grace that calms our fears.
Each heartbeat sings a sacred song,
In every trial, we still belong.

Let kindness mark the road we tread,
With gentle hearts, we forge ahead.
In trials faced or joys embraced,
We see Your love, forever placed.

With open eyes, we learn and grow,
In every act, Your truth will show.
From dawn to dusk, Your light will gleam,
Each moment lived, a living dream.

As shadows fall, we stand united,
In hope's embrace, we are ignited.
Every moment, Lord, our song,
In faith we walk, where we belong.

Threads of Hope Woven Daily

With every dawn, new threads are spun,
In tapestry, life is begun.
With colors rich, our spirits rise,
In love and truth, we realize.

Each thread of hope, in patience sewn,
In fields of grace, our faith has grown.
Together weaving dreams so bright,
In unity, we share the light.

As challenges come, we stand as one,
Through every storm, we see the sun.
For in the fabric of our days,
Hope binds us close, in countless ways.

Let every thread of kindness flow,
In hearts and hands where love can grow.
With every stitch, our voices blend,
In harmony, we shall not bend.

So let us weave, through joy and strife,
A testament of sacred life.
In every moment, love displayed,
Threads of hope, we've bravely laid.

Faithful Steps

In the shadow of the mountains, I tread,
Guided by the whispers, softly said.
Each step I take, a promise made,
With every heartbeat, my fears do fade.

The path is narrow, but light shall lead,
Through valleys deep, where faith is freed.
Though storms may rage and darkness loom,
In trust, I find my spirit's bloom.

I walk with hope, hand in hand with grace,
In every trial, I see His face.
Each stumble turns to lessons learned,
From ashes rise, my spirit burned.

With faithful steps, I journey on,
Each sunrise brightens—a brand new dawn.
In prayer, I find my solace true,
A sacred bond, forever new.

So onward, through the night I roam,
In every heart, I find my home.
With every breath, I feel His call,
In faithful steps, I'll never fall.

Bread for Today

Give us this day our humble bread,
In gratitude for all we've said.
With every crumb, a gift divine,
Sustaining hearts in love's design.

The table set, a feast to share,
In unity, we lift our prayer.
Nourished by Your grace, we live,
In every moment, in every forgive.

Lord, fill our hearts with joyful song,
In Your embrace, we all belong.
Each meal a blessing, richly bestowed,
In gratitude, our spirits flowed.

When shadows fall and hope seems thin,
Your light shines bright, it draws us in.
We gather close, in faith we stay,
With bread for today, we find our way.

In sharing love, we break the crust,
In every bite, we place our trust.
For in this feast, we find our role,
Bread for today, it fills the soul.

Grace in the Morning Light

As dawn awakens, grace descends,
With every ray, a love that mends.
In morning light, my spirit stirs,
Embraced by truth, the heart concurs.

With every breath, a chance to see,
The beauty of His majesty.
In quiet whispers, hope ignites,
Guiding my soul through starry nights.

The world anew, the day begins,
With grace, our journey never ends.
In all we do, His love abounds,
In gentle peace, true joy is found.

Through trials faced, His mercy flows,
In fields of grace, our spirit grows.
With every step, my heart takes flight,
In harmony, we find delight.

So let us rise in morning's glow,
Embrace the light, let love bestow.
With grace, we walk this path so bright,
In every moment, in His sight.

Daily Bread

In the rhythm of each passing day,
I seek Your face, Your gentle way.
With daily bread, my spirit fed,
In love and faith, I forge ahead.

The simple gifts that You provide,
In every heart, Your truth resides.
In humble thanks, I bow my head,
For every crumb, my soul's in depth.

As morning breaks and shadows flee,
I find my strength, my God in Thee.
Each meal a blessing, richly shared,
In gratitude, I find I'm bared.

The hands that give, the hearts that share,
In unity, we learn to care.
Together, in His light, we stand,
With daily bread, a loving hand.

From trials faced, to laughter bright,
We gather strength, in love's pure light.
With every bite, we dare to pray,
That daily bread shows us the way.

Daily Blessings

In the dawn of each new day, we rise,
With hearts open wide to the skies.
Count our blessings, both big and small,
In gratitude, we give our all.

Each smile shared, each kind embrace,
In fleeting moments, we find grace.
With thankful hearts, we walk in peace,
In daily blessings, our joys increase.

Through trials faced and roads unclear,
We find His presence ever near.
In faith we trust, in love we soar,
With daily blessings, we seek for more.

Each breath a gift, each laugh a light,
In unity, our spirits unite.
With every step, we share love's song,
In daily blessings, we all belong.

Through all we face, we know it's true,
With every trial, He makes us new.
In humble hearts, His love does dwell,
In daily blessings, all is well.

In the Shadow of Each Sunrise

In the dawn's gentle embrace,
Hope awakens, bathed in grace.
Whispers of dreams carried high,
Under the vast, unbroken sky.

As light breaks the darkness apart,
A new day's blessing ignites the heart.
Each hue paints a sacred song,
Guiding our spirits, where we belong.

In the quiet of morning's sigh,
Faith ignites, like stars up high.
Through trials that life does send,
Love will guide us, never to end.

The sun rises, a promise anew,
Reminding us what we must pursue.
In every shadow, His love we find,
As we walk forth, His truths in mind.

Life unfolds in nature's beat,
With every step, His mercy we greet.
In the shadow of the day's first light,
We flourish, bold, with hearts so bright.

Today's Miracle

Each breath a gift, a sacred chance,
In nature's rhythm, we find our dance.
Every moment, a chance to see,
The wonders that set our spirits free.

Sunrise glimmers, hope takes flight,
Miracles bloom in the softest light.
In kindness shared, or laughter's grace,
We find the spark of the Divine embrace.

Hearts joined together in love's sweet song,
Right here is where we all belong.
Each gentle act, a seed we sow,
Today's miracle begins to grow.

With open eyes, we greet the day,
Thankful for blessings that come our way.
In every smile, in every tear,
God's presence lingers, always near.

So let us cherish what life has planned,
With grateful hearts, hand in hand.
In today's miracle, let us find,
The shine of love, both pure and kind.

Blessings Counted at Dusk

As day retreats, the sun dips low,
We gather 'round the evening's glow.
With thankful hearts, we take our pause,
Echoing His kindness, for this cause.

In whispers soft, we count our grace,
In memories cherished, we find our place.
Each blessing shared, a tapestry spun,
Threads of light woven, we've all won.

In the twilight's calm, we bow in prayer,
For moments lived and love laid bare.
With each star a promise, shining bright,
Guiding our souls through the tender night.

Let us remember the joy we've known,
In trials faced, in seeds we've sown.
At dusk, when shadows begin to rise,
We find His mercy beneath the skies.

So gather close, let love abound,
In harmony, let our hearts be found.
Counting blessings under evening's glow,
In the stillness, His spirit flows.

The Path of Trust

In the journey of faith, we tread each day,
With courage and hearts that softly sway.
Hand in hand, we walk this road,
Trusting in Him to lighten the load.

The path is winding, the skies may gray,
Yet in our hearts, hope finds a way.
Through storms and trials, we hold on tight,
His love a lantern, our guiding light.

With every step, we learn to see,
The beauty in pain, the strength to be free.
In moments of doubt, in shadows cast,
We whisper His name, our fears surpassed.

Together we rise, with faith in our veins,
Believing His promise in joys and pains.
Though the road may twist, like branches entwined,
We walk in trust, His grace defined.

So let us embrace what lies ahead,
With open hearts where love is spread.
The path of trust leads us home,
In every heartbeat, we are never alone.